YOUR KNOWLEDGE HAS VALUE

- We will publish your bachelor's and master's thesis, essays and papers

- Your own eBook and book - sold worldwide in all relevant shops

- Earn money with each sale

Upload your text at www.GRIN.com
and publish for free

Bibliographic information published by the German National Library:

The German National Library lists this publication in the National Bibliography; detailed bibliographic data are available on the Internet at http://dnb.dnb.de .

This book is copyright material and must not be copied, reproduced, transferred, distributed, leased, licensed or publicly performed or used in any way except as specifically permitted in writing by the publishers, as allowed under the terms and conditions under which it was purchased or as strictly permitted by applicable copyright law. Any unauthorized distribution or use of this text may be a direct infringement of the author s and publisher s rights and those responsible may be liable in law accordingly.

Imprint:

Copyright © 2018 GRIN Verlag
Print and binding: Books on Demand GmbH, Norderstedt Germany
ISBN: 9783668683419

This book at GRIN:

https://www.grin.com/document/419695

Adrian Tamayo, Florence R. Magistrado

Service Satisfaction Survey of Regional Health Services for 2016

GRIN Verlag

GRIN - Your knowledge has value

Since its foundation in 1998, GRIN has specialized in publishing academic texts by students, college teachers and other academics as e-book and printed book. The website www.grin.com is an ideal platform for presenting term papers, final papers, scientific essays, dissertations and specialist books.

Visit us on the internet:

http://www.grin.com/

http://www.facebook.com/grincom

http://www.twitter.com/grin_com

2016 Service Satisfaction Survey of Regional Health Services XI[1]

Adrian M. Tamayo*, PCI Florence R. Magistrado**

*Research Director, Research and Publication Center, University of Mindanao, Matina, Davao City
** Hospital Administrator, Regional Health Services XI, Camp Quintin Merecido, Catitipan, Buhangin, Davao City

ABSTRACT 2
INTRODUCTION 2
OBJECTIVES 3
METHOD 3
RESULTS 3
CONCLUSION and RECOMMENDATIONS 8
REFERENCES 1

---

[1] This study is pursuant to the Memorandum of Agreement signed between the University of Mindanao and the Regional Health Services XI of the Philippine National Police.

ABSTRACT

The service quality of Regional Health Services can generally be assessed by tangibles, empathy and competence, and promptness of services. The tangibles refers to the satisfaction on the cleanliness of the ward, proper lighting and ventilation of rooms, adequacy of provisions for safety; the empathy and competence refers to the skills of the doctors and the nurses, their understanding of the illness and management of it; while the promptness refers to the availability of ambulance services and availability of bed covers. The promptness dimension needs to be improved.

In particular, the study determined 5 dimensions of service quality: professional services of doctors, professional services of nurses, efficiency and effectiveness, physical support, and provision of safety and precaution. The Regional Health Services, as a whole, enjoyed very high satisfaction ratings, by indicator; it posted outstanding rating in physical support services. Dimension needing immediate attention is efficiency and effectiveness.

Importance analysis further identified dimensions that have huge impact on satisfaction. These are efficiency & effectiveness, provision of safety and precaution, and the professional services of the doctor.

Keywords: health service, dimensions of quality

INTRODUCTION

Service quality measurement is an important barometer of the overall success of an organization[1]. Commonly, it measures the opinions of the managers and the stakeholders of the organization[2]. Hospitals and health service organizations are not exemptions to this. Van Damme & Leunis (1993)[3] demand the inclusion of criteria for organizational success, the service quality. In Hong Kong, the opinions of the patients take considerable share in the assessment of the services of hospitals[4]. Quality of health service, be it a private or public, is an important consideration in order to achieve quality workforce. More often, individuals avoid availing health service because of its associated cost[5]. Choices pursued by the individuals are selective health service, those they see as cost-effective and efficient in delivery.

Hospital service providers measure quality service using the two-pronged lens of technical quality and functional quality[6]. Accordingly, the former refers to the accuracy of diagnoses and procedures while the latter means quality of the health care provided to the patients. In addition, ServQual (Service Quality) dimensions were added as sub-dimensions to health service quality. These include, among others, responsiveness, competence, understanding or empathy, and tangibles[7].

OBJECTIVES

This study aimed to determine the level of satisfaction on the services of the Regional Health Services XI. In particular, the study aimed to determine highly rated dimensions and evaluate these relative to established quality service measures. Likewise, low rated dimensions were identified and evaluated.

METHOD

A survey was conducted among the beneficiary of the Regional Health Services XI. A total of 100 respondents were surveyed. The questionnaire generally convey measurement on professional services divided into doctors and nurses, efficiency and effectiveness measurement, physical support measurement and safety & precautions.

Table 1
Scale range and description

Lower bound	Upper bound	Description
4.3	5	Outstanding
3.5	4.2	Very satisfactory
2.7	3.4	Satisfactory
1.9	2.6	Poor
1.0	1.8	Needs Improvement

RESULTS

Respondents were found to be very satisfied (4.18) with the professional services of the doctor. Said level of satisfaction is attributable to the skills demonstrated by the doctor to the patients (4.24), which also bears concern and the right attitude towards them (4.24). However, one thing that would need attention, although very minimal in nature, is the time spent by the doctor (4.04). Either this refers to the frequency of rounds much like in any other hospitals, or the time spent talking and explaining to the patient the illness. At any rate, it is an area of improvement. See details presented in table 2.

Table 2
Satisfaction on the Professional Services, Doctor

Indicators	Mean	Description
Skills	4.24	Very satisfactory
Time spent	4.04	Very satisfactory
Concern and attitude	4.24	Very satisfactory
Education on illness & management	4.18	Very satisfactory
Mean	4.18	Very satisfactory

Satisfaction of professional services was also rated very satisfactorily (4.09) which is described heavily by their very satisfactory assessment of the concern and attitude manifested by the nurse (4.19) and the education on illness and management (4.11). However, though a concern is evident, the respondents still pointed out the skills as an area of improvement (4.01), yet the rating is something not to be anxious about. See table 3.

Table 3
Satisfaction on Professional Services, Nurse

Indicators	Mean	Description
Concern and attitude	4.19	Very satisfactory
Skills	4.01	Very satisfactory
Education on illness & management	4.11	Very satisfactory
Promptness in attending to needs	4.03	Very satisfactory
Mean	4.09	Very satisfactory

The ability of the doctors and the nurses to respond to the needs of the patients, as well as show concern to them is deemed empathy dimension in the parlance of management and marketing[8]. For one, the empathy of the nurses makes impacts on the satisfaction of the patients[10].

Another dimension for satisfaction assessment is the effectiveness and efficiency. This refers to the actual service delivery and the post-hospital services such as reimbursement. Though rated with a pull-back (3.93), it is still within the scale of very satisfactory range. The pull-back is due to the low ratings on availability of the ambulance service (3.62) and the availability of the bed covers (3.70). This is quite interesting to note. Given that there is a hospital, it is logical to think of an ambulance, its availability and adequacy of an ambulance service. In addition, bed covers are fundamental in a hospital. Perhaps, this is the nature of the hospital services provided to the PNP personnel, to require them to bring their own covers. Yet, it is just appropriate for the hospital to maintain an effective and responsive housekeeping section.

Post-hospitalization services were recognized by the respondents, the timeliness and completeness of medicine obtained highest rating (4.14) followed by the reimbursements (4.10). Still closely behind is the satisfaction that the hospital provides right diet, quality and quantity of food to the patients. See table 4.

Table 4
Satisfaction on hospital services

Effectiveness and efficiency	Mean	Description
Right diet, quality and quantity of foods	4.09	Very satisfactory
Reimbursement is made	4.10	Very satisfactory
Timeliness and completeness of medicine	4.14	Very satisfactory
Availability of bed covers	3.70	Very satisfactory
Availability of ambulance service	3.62	Very satisfactory
Mean	3.93	Very satisfactory

Satisfaction on physical support posted an outstanding rating (4.26). The cleanliness of the comfort room and bathroom obtained very high ratings (4.26). The cleanliness of the ward, the ventilation and the lighting was also rated outstanding (4.25). See table 5.

Table 5
Satisfaction on hospital services, physical support

Physical support services	Mean	Description
Ward/room is clean, lighted and well-ventilated	4.25	Outstanding
Cleanliness of comfort room/bathroom	4.26	Outstanding
Mean	4.26	Outstanding

Table 6 presents the satisfaction ratings indicated by the 100 respondents on the safety and precautionary provisions. On the whole, this dimension was rated very satisfactorily (4.22) due to the highly yet closely rated items like provision of luggage room (4.24), fire extinguisher (4.21) and side rails (4.20) to assist patients' movement and mobility.

Table 6
Satisfaction on hospital services, provision of safety and precautions

Provision of safety and precaution	Mean	Description
side rails	4.20	Very satisfactory
fire extinguisher	4.21	Very satisfactory
luggage room	4.24	Very satisfactory
Mean	4.22	Very satisfactory

Thus, a summary of the dimensions was presented in figure 1. Notably, the efficiency and effectiveness measurement fell below at 3.9. This is indicative for the need to improve or find measures to improve service satisfaction. In particular, the services of the ambulance may be improved. Also, a housekeeping section might be reviewed with the intention of evaluating readiness to respond to influx of patients.

Physical support obtained the outstanding rating (4.3), followed by the professional services of doctor and the provisions of safety and precautionary measures both obtained a very satisfactory rating (4.20). This is contrary to studies conducted in other countries, where physical expectations came out to be lowest (Lam, 1997). Perhaps, the hospital is at its best physical quality compared to other hospitals that the patients can compare with.

A non-stochastic statistical analysis was conducted to determine which of the dimensions would have significant impact on the level of satisfaction on the services of the RHS XI. Of the five dimensions, highest importance value was obtained for efficiency and services (see column indicating importance), followed by safety and precautionary measures (0.20). See table 7

However, the normalized process which indicate the normalized value that would show degree of importance of each dimension to the whole satisfaction rating, it was observed that the efficiency services have a 100% importance degree. This means that the said dimension maintains very huge, if not all, contribution to the improvement of satisfaction of services. This is being followed by the safety and precautionary, followed by the doctor professional service, to complete the ranking of the top 3 most important areas of satisfaction. See figure 2 for the graphical presentation.

Table 7
Independent Variable Importance Analysis Using Artificial Neural Analysis

Indicators	Importance	Normalized Importance
Doctor Professional Services	0.19	64.63
Nurse Professional Services	0.18	62.58
Efficiency & Effectiveness	0.29	100.00
Physical support	0.13	45.91
Safety and precautionary	0.20	68.34

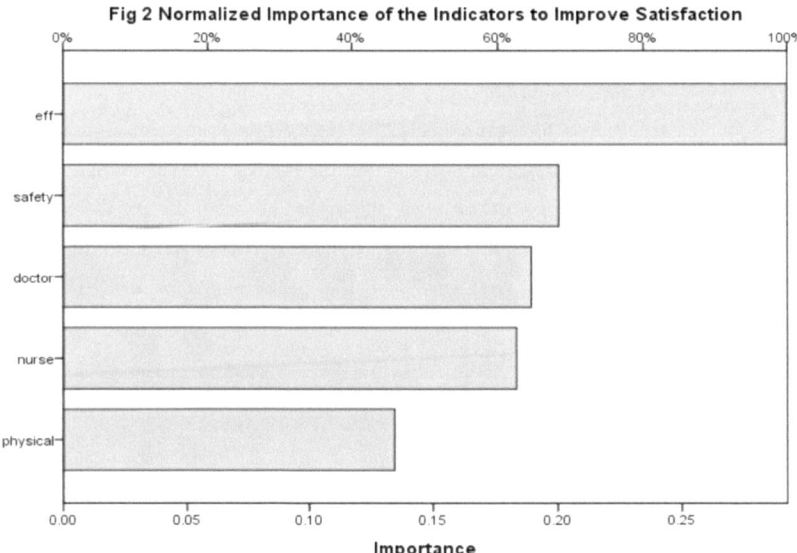

CONCLUSION and RECOMMENDATIONS

Given the following findings, it was noted that the satisfaction of the respondents are generally and primarily associated with the tangibles. The tangibles include a clean ward, proper ventilation and lighting. These are those that are seen and readily observable. Secondary service quality dimension of the RHS is empathy and competence of the professional. Though here, has reference to the services of the doctor. The responsiveness dimension came out also as equally important. This refers to the provision of side rails for mobility, a luggage room and the fire extinguisher.

Importance analysis further identified dimensions that have huge impact on satisfaction. These are efficiency & effectiveness, provision of safety and precaution, and the professional services of the doctor.

In particular ambulance services and the availability of bed covers receive interesting ratings, which is a biting wit in the operation of a health service or in a hospital in particular. Thus, it is recommended that there should be on stand-by personnel to man the ambulance, 24/7. Also, review of the housekeeping policy must be initiated to address the gap on the availability of bed covers.

Moreover, it is recommended that the questionnaire for the satisfaction survey be re-calibrated to follow pattern of indicators as revealed in the study. Such that the survey questionnaire can now be widely grouped to 4 indicators of professional services of doctor and nurse, efficiency and effectiveness, physical support services, and provision of safety and precaution.

Finally, as a matter of continuous quality improvement, it is recommended that the RHS will determine a threshold score. Given the results, a threshold may be set at 4.0, such that, target ratings must be at or above the threshold for the Calendar Year 2017. Likewise, It is recommended that the satisfaction survey must be continued in order to obtain comparable assessment of the performance of the RHS over a determined period of time.

REFERENCES

[1] McAlexander, J. H., Kaldenburg, D. O., & Koenig, H. F. (1994). Service quality measurement. *Marketing Health Services*, *14*(3), 34.

[2] Lewis, B. R. (1993). Service quality measurement. *Marketing Intelligence & Planning*, *11*(4), 4-12.

[3] Vandamme, R., & Leunis, J. (1993). Development of a multiple-item scale for measuring hospital service quality. *International Journal of Service Industry Management*, *4*(3), 30-49.

[4] Lam, S. S. (1997). SERVQUAL: A tool for measuring patients' opinions of hospital service quality in Hong Kong. *Total Quality Management*, *8*(4), 145-152.

[5] Andaleeb, S. S. (2001). Service quality perceptions and patient satisfaction: a study of hospitals in a developing country. *Social science & medicine*, *52*(9), 1359-1370.

[6] Babakus, E., & Mangold, W. G. (1992). Adapting the SERVQUAL scale to hospital services: an empirical investigation. *Health services research*, *26*(6), 767.

[7] Papanikolaou, V., & Zygiaris, S. (2014). Service quality perceptions in primary health care centres in Greece. *Health expectations*, *17*(2), 197-207.

[8] Tamayo, A. M. (2011). Psychographic measure of service quality of fastfood chain in Davao city. *African Journal of Marketing Management*, *3*(9), 219-225.

[9] Boshoff, C., & Gray, B. (2004). The relationships between service quality, customer satisfaction and buying intentions in the private hospital industry. *South African journal of business management*, *35*(4), 27-37.

[10] Wisniewski, M., & Wisniewski, H. (2005). Measuring service quality in a hospital colposcopy clinic. *International Journal of Health Care Quality Assurance*, *18*(3), 217-228.

YOUR KNOWLEDGE HAS VALUE

- We will publish your bachelor's and master's thesis, essays and papers

- Your own eBook and book - sold worldwide in all relevant shops

- Earn money with each sale

Upload your text at www.GRIN.com
and publish for free